Enjoy

by Toshiki Okada

English translation
by Aya Ogawa

D1601588

A SAMUEL FRENCH ACTING EDITION

SAMUEL
FRENCH
FOUNDED 1830

NEW YORK HOLLYWOOD LONDON TORONTO

SAMUELFRENCH.COM

ISBN 978-0-573-69959-7   Printed in U.S.A.   #29992

MUSIC USE NOTE

Licensees are solely responsible for obtaining formal written permission from copyright owners to use copyrighted music in the performance of this play and are strongly cautioned to do so. If no such permission is obtained by the licensee, then the licensee must use only original music that the licensee owns and controls. Licensees are solely responsible and liable for all music clearances and shall indemnify the copyright owners of the play and their licensing agent, Samuel French, Inc., against any costs, expenses, losses and liabilities arising from the use of music by licensees.

IMPORTANT BILLING AND CREDIT
REQUIREMENTS

All producers of *ENJOY must* give credit to the Authors of the Play in all programs distributed in connection with performances of the Play, and in all instances in which the title of the Play appears for the purposes of advertising, publicizing or otherwise exploiting the Play and/or a production. The name of the Authors *must* appear on a separate line on which no other name appears, immediately following the title and *must* appear in size of type not less than fifty percent of the size of the title type.

In addition the following credit *must* be given in all programs and publicity information distributed in association with this piece:

This translation was originally commissioned and developed by
The Play Company,
(Kate Loewald, Founding Producer) in New York City

ENJOY was first produced by The Play Company at 59E59 in New York City on March 27, 2010. The performance was directed by Dan Rothenberg, with sets by Mimi Lien, costumes by Maiko Matsushima, lighting by James Clotfelter, and sound by Daniel Kluger. The Production Stage Manager was Dave Polato. The cast was as follows:

ACTOR 1	Kris Kling
ACTOR 2	Frank Harts
ACTRESS 1	Kira Sternbach
ACTOR 3	Steven Boyer
ACTOR 4	Joseph Midyett
ACTOR 5	Alex Torra
ACTRESS 2	Stacey Yen
ACTRESS 3	Mary McCool
ACTRESS 4	Jessica Almasy
ACTOR 6	Joshua Koehn

CHARACTERS

ACTOR 1

ACTOR 2

ACTRESS 1

ACTOR 3

ACTOR 4

ACTRESS 2

ACTRESS 3

ACTOR 5

ACTRESS 4

ACTOR 6

"Since the beginning of 2002, the Japanese economy has entered into a period of full-fledged resurgence, and despite flagging export and production in the autumn of 2004, by mid-2005 it has stabilized and continued to recover. Employment conditions were such that by June of 2005, the unemployment rate was down to 4.2%. New job opportunities and job-to-applicant ratios continued to rise. As the economic climate continues to warm up, hiring accruals and wage increases are expected to rise as well; however the prevalent standard model heretofore of the uniform distribution of achievements among the labor force has been shifting over time. The number of part-time workers, freelancers, contracted employees, temps, short-term employees and others who fall outside of conventional economic standing have drastically increased, creating a diverse work environment but also decreasing regular employment. With the upswing of the economy, there has been an increase of graduating students heading straight for full-time employment and a decrease in young unemployed and freelancers; however, there are still an increasing number of temp workers among the younger generation, and this denormalized work climate continues to grow. For those young workers who were affected by the bursting of the bubble economy, which resulted in cutbacks on hiring and an extremely competitive job market, it is becoming increasingly difficult to move towards a regularized employment climate. While hopping from one part-time position to another, they scrambled to stay afloat in an unstable work climate, with an increasing unemployment rate, and this generation has grown older. "Long-time part-timers" were seen as unlikely to hold onto jobs for a long time, lacking in career ambition, and the generation of young people "Not in Education, Employment or Training" (aka NEET) are now growing older. Even if they are able to obtain a full-time position, depending on the field they are in, there is a big difference in their ability to improve job skills."

(from a white paper published by The Ministry of Health, Labor and Welfare in Heisei 15 [2006])

ACT ONE: A STAFF ROOM IN A MANGA (COMIC BOOK) CAFE

(There is a mop upstage.)

ACTOR 1. We'll begin with Act One… This guy named Kato was riding the subway the other day, he was riding the Keio line and, he had an encounter then, when he sat next to… There were these two women who were talking, but… Kato had no intention of eavesdropping at all, of course but, while he was listening, to be honest, he… in the end, from the middle of the conversation, it did turn completely into eavesdropping but… you know how for text messaging they have those screen stickers that you put on your phone to keep your screen hidden from the person standing next to you, well, there aren't such things for voices, so in a way, it's a little like too bad, you know, which may be like totally an excuse but… but with that conversation, it was a little like no matter how you look at it, their voices were, clearly above and beyond what is a standard volume, I mean, come on, was the way it seemed and that was because… on top of that the content of the conversation itself also like, would have piqued anyone's interest in this…

ACTOR 1. But, never mind about that story, I mean we'll get into it later, let's just put it aside for now, so I have to tell the story about what happened before he got on the train, when he went into the bathroom at the station, I mean it's not like I *have* to but do you mind?

ACTOR 1. So like, the thing about what was that bathroom was, of course it was the men's but, there was the thing for the number one and the thing for the number two, and at that moment I was there for the

number one to… the number one, and the area for
the number one was, you know how there's like this
row all along the wall for the places to do number one,
at that moment it wasn't that crowded but, in fact, it
was just me in there, doing my business, positioned in
like the middle of this huge row along the wall and…
then to my back, see, on the other side, in the bathroom at this station, of course I don't know how the
women's side is but, in the men's there are all these
private stalls for the number two like lined up in a row
just like the number one guys but in a separate area,
if the number ones guys were lined up in a row like
this, then the area for the number two stalls would be
kind of at like a 90 degree angle to it and, there was a
man in there and, I mean it was totally fine that he was
in there but… this man came out but, I mean it was
fine that he came out but, he came out of there with
a "swoosh"… it's not that he was saying "swoosh" with
his mouth, but he came out after flushing the water
"swoosh," and then really… normally, with common
sense you'd think "oh, this guy's gonna just wash his
hands and leave, right?" um, am I wrong? …But then
really, this guy made this super-mysterious move from
there… my, for some reason, he comes to the urinal
right next to my urinal, and suddenly there starts with
the number one, "psssssss"

ACTOR 2. Oh, right on, right on,

(**ACTOR 2** *is holding an unopened carton of cigarettes.*)

ACTOR 2. …So then in that moment, Kato was, basically he
was looking at this dude who'd come out of the booth,
or like stall and was thinking "Huh? then why didn't
you take care of that number one together with your
other stuff inside just now," and,

ACTOR 1. This person *(indicating* **ACTOR 2***)* is named
Kawakami but… on first impression you might think
that particularly his reaction to the punch line part of
Kato's story seemed totally slow, but,

ACTOR 2. But that's not the case, to tell you the truth, Kawakami at that moment was thinking, "But occasionally I do stuff like that, and by stuff like that I mean re-considering after I'm out of the stall, 'Oh, I want to push out a little more after all on the number one side of things,'" I mean thinking back I have a keen sense of that kind of thing, I remember physically, a lot of different times and episodes in my memory, all like spinning around, and similar to that story, and recalling them, I got distracted, so that's the reason my reaction was flat,

ACTOR 2. But honestly, huh, haven't you even once done something like that? I um have, is what Kawakami was thinking,

ACTOR 2. ...Right right... I can even recall now, 1, 2, 3, 4 times, except if someone were to interrogate me like, "Come on, what was the deal there?" like, why I did that at those times, probably, now, I can't think of a convincing answer to, I mean, I can't remember every single miniscule detail of that situation so,

ACTOR 1. Uh-uh, that's like totally fine,

ACTOR 2. Even if I were perhaps asked to convince you with a clear explanation, I don't think that I could but,

ACTOR 1. It's like, OK, I understand that... Things like that happen, right... Well, it's not like things like that happen but... huh, but so Kawakami, you have done things like that, a lot of times?

ACTOR 2. Or like, if you ask me if I've done it "a lot of times," it might like be misleading but, it's not so much like I go use the bathroom in the station every-day or anything,

ACTOR 1. But, wow, right, that means that someone who's actually experienced this phenomenon is like surpris-ingly close-by... what kind of, uh, but when you're in that circumstance, in a situation that might turn out like that... so then, practically speaking, for that to happen... for example is it like after you've already flushed once, "Oh, actually I just recognized, and in this very moment, that there is a part of myself that needed to go, actually," or something like that? Is what I'm asking as a general question, but…

ACTOR 2. …Right, right… or like, to use a subtle analogy, there's like in all these different power dynamics, from moment to moment… like the relationships between the particulars of a circumstance, that on one level… like time, for example, fundamentally, when you're in a train station, you're in a hurry, that's like the standard assumption, right, and that is like one possible factor that could affect circumstances, and when you bring all these different contributing factors together, that's when…. right, right… that kind of thing happens, but it's really delicate, and even though it's not like that isn't categorically THE logic, on one level,

ACTOR 1. Ah, yes, yes,

ACTOR 2. But… right, right… but if you're trying to understand something by that logic alone, like that black-and-white kind of thinking, the second you make a decision, there's always somewhere a doorway into thinking, "Oh, but that's a little bit like maybe not totally right either I wonder"…. right, right,… the lingering thought, which on some level, like, there's nothing you can do about it, but there's a, it's too bad, like kind of thing, right… but on the other hand those kinds of doing something without leaving any loose ends, like the perfect crime, that in and of itself would be on the other hand, a pretty difficult task in its own right, I think, so,

ACTOR 1. …and so right when we were getting all excited by this topic which the two of us had gradually lost track of, … I think you get it from what you're watching but, so a girl enters here, right, and so she comes in here, I mean it's not like "what the hell are you doing, coming in here" or anything like that at all, I mean it's totally fine if she comes in but,

ACTOR 1. And the reason behind that is because, the circumstances were, in other words, to explain where this place is… in Shinjuku, Shinjuku is the urban center, I mean all of Tokyo is urban, but it's kind of like the epicenter of Tokyo, kind of like Times Square, and that's where this comic book café is, in the middle of Shinjuku, I mean, the whole first three floors of this building is a karaoke place, and the entire fourth and fifth floors are this comic cafe, and that's where Kato and Kawakami and this girl, who's called Ogawa… all work part-time but, this is the break room or changing room kind of, that can lock from the inside, I mean, the door can be locked from the inside but, this room here is what is commonly called the staff room, and that is where at that moment Ogawa just entered so…. Of course Ogawa has every right, Ogawa is still pretty new here, one of the newest, who started working here only about one week ago, but, anyway, even still it's totally fine if she comes in here all normal, but that doesn't have to do with anything but,

ACTOR 2. Except this is when, there's this thing that's a little story about Ogawa, or like it just so happens to be break time coincidentally, when Ogawa happened to come in, and it was a perfect opportunity so… Right right, there was this thing I was thinking maybe I'll just dare to ask her now,

ACTRESS 1. Huh? Is this about Mizuno?

ACTOR 2. …or rather, as far as Ogawa was concerned, honestly, we were at that point perpetually ready to get all excited at the drop of a hat, and so… or rather, with Mizuno… right, right… the reason why was, what happened was…. the thing with Mizuno… right, right…. there was this ahhh- I was just totally BANG preempted, right, the thing is, first of all Ogawa is, above all, a fresh college graduate this spring, 22 years old, an age that's, I mean to put it bluntly, very young is the thing, right, except we weren't necessarily getting all excited over just her babe-liciousness… the important point here is something else… I mean that is, well, on the other hand, as a detail, there was a level at which we were just getting excited, and that of course is like the perpetuation of our seed, that because we are men, I think it should be admitted here, on one level, we have that which all men have, to be honest, because we're men, or like because we're men, since we've acknowledged that, ok, so we can continue the story fairly… the fact is, there is a group of us who're pretty tight, all the same age, to be honest, there's this, me and Kato and plus one other part-timer, the guy Ogawa mentioned earlier but, a guy named Mizuno, and this Mizuno… so then, it's that, right, the way that it wasn't that we were just getting excited over Ogawa because she was "just so young, you know," but practically speaking… something, not exactly like a felony but, on the other hand, it was like this huge feat had taken place, where, Ogawa, believe it or not, and Mizuno, of all people, were like, as I said,

ACTOR 2. …Uh, the fact that you, Ogawa, were kind of like, to put it bluntly, asked by Mizuno to like "go out" with him, and the fact that you OK'ed it, uh, you OK'ed it right, huh? Hey, is the fact that you OK'ed it, like a final answer, or maybe it was actually a fast break, type thing, maybe? Looking at the actual circumstances, in other words, I think you were actually asked something similar by Mizuno,

ACTRESS 1. Huh – yes,

ACTOR 2. In that moment, did you feel it was a pretty much relatively momentarily like it was a snap decision? is what I'm trying to say,

ACTRESS 1. Huh – but it wasn't really that, huh, why is it like, huh, the way you, Kawakami, put it just now, makes it sound so fakey, so is that what the story is? is what it feels like but, I wonder, huh, is that what people are saying?

ACTOR 2. Oh, but that was just, it's probably totally fine so…

ACTRESS 1. I mean that it was from Mizuno's side? Only? It wasn't just a one-way thing, or like, uh, did that come out really lame? I wondered for a moment but, uh, what should I say, I mean, whatever is fine, but

ACTOR 2. I mean, that's totally… right, right… You probably don't need to worry about it at all right now, because, to be honest, Kato and I are getting pretty excited about it, regarding you and Mizuno but, when you look at it another way, we're probably the only people getting all worked up about it, is the feeling I get so…

ACTRESS 1. Huh – the way Kawakami said that like that was like, it made me think, at this part-time job, stuff like this rumor about how apparently Mizuno's approach was totally one-sided or, huh, but why is that? The story? I totally don't understand it but, are rumors and things just like that? is what I thought, or like, that lies are, uh, so out of control, huh, how excited are you getting, over other peoples' business? is what I totally, in reality – you have to look to understand but, uh, is this perhaps some bizarre story that is getting all the staff at the store, all excited, because it feels like that would be really weird, or huh, I dunno, I mean, it's fine, but,

ACTRESS 1. That's what Ogawa was thinking but, it seemed like, in reality, nobody was getting all excited about it actually, so, well if it was not like everyone was getting all worked up about it, then everything that just went through my head is all irrelevant, right,

ACTOR 2. In other words, it's not so… right, right… don't worry because I'm, we're not making a like party out of it or anything, and I say don't worry, I mean, for Ogawa's part, I could tell that it wasn't as if she didn't want things to get weirdly excited, or, that she was like phew! that people weren't all excited, in fact, it was obvious that the exact opposite was true but… right, right… as a bystander the only thing I could really say was "Don't worry" so, it just had to come out like that but…

ACTRESS 1. It's not completely accurate to say, that I don't want people to get excited over something pertaining to me, uh, but see, the key point maybe is that there's a feeling that if I could choose what got people excited, then I would want to choose, is, I mean of course it's normal that you can't do that... But, huh am I weird? Like I feel like the age difference factor was way over-blown more than was necessary... Well, uh, do people really make that the focal point when they get all excited? Isn't that a little, hmmm, or like first of all, it isn't like there even is an age difference worth men-tioning, in my opinion but, am I the only person who thinks that? Or like is it just us? I mean whatever but,

ACTOR 1. Totally, if we're talking about that particular point, the three of us, including Mizuno, we're treated like a trio, and honestly, easily half of all the other staff, including the full-timers and the part-timers, are totally in their twenties so, hmmmmm, even though there is something pathetic about this kind of assertion, still... After all, when you look at the part-time work situa-tion in its entirety, and then at the three of us...we're pretty even though nobody says it to our faces, there is this subtle feeling like we are made out to be the three musketeers in their 30's, and labeled the old fogey trio, and despite that, we still have to work here part-time, from day to day so, awwwww... you understand that feeling, right? I mean since Ogawa and Mizuno are already like you know, so... or like, isn't it safe for us to assume that if you spent one week working here, you'd understand that there's that kind of atmosphere in our store, right?

ACTOR 1. Right, so it's pretty, at times, this person might in reality have absolutely no idea what the other per-son's side is feeling but, have you not heard this story from Mizuno? Or like even if you haven't, haven't you actually thought that? on some level, you actually have, right?

ACTRESS 1. Uh...but this is, I'm not trying to sound cool or anything, but truthfully, I'm not at all like doing that kind of thing *(fighting the world)* but... uh- is age difference such a big deal?

ACTOR 2. Or like, the age difference thing is, yeah, more like OUR problem, kind of, and by OUR problem that includes Mizuno, and so before you realize it, there are these issues about what kind of position one takes, and where you stand now, I mean aren't these the kinds of issues that ought to be discussed with Ogawa? Or like... right, right.... so Ogawa from the beginning or like even today but, or like more so now than ever but, when we are in the staff room, Ogawa is the only person who normally comes in here on a regular basis, and everyone else, when we're inside here, probably goes out of their way to go to the convenience store, you know...

ACTOR 2. Despite the fact that we're right smack in the middle of Shinjuku here, you actually have to walk pretty far to get to a convenience store, and I think that's extremely annoying but... but they go there anyway, which means that they must really you know, so because of that, from our point of view, Ogawa is practically, I mean not to get all religious but, the Virgin Mary or like, actually, I don't know but she's on that level, you know, and I have a feeling that's not such a wild exaggeration, how can I put it... Right, right, also, who was that, that woman from India, but she's not really Indian, what's her name, she's already dead but...

ACTOR 1. The other people here don't come in here casually when we're in here, because they're already naturally fixed in that culture... that's why we... But Ogawa, she comes in here right, and in the beginning, because it was before we knew anything about her and Mizuno, or rather, there was of course a time before anything was actually happening between them so, during that time, we were like, Ah- It's because Ogawa is still a newbie who hasn't completely absorbed all the cultural nuances of our work place, isn't that nice? It's comforting, isn't it, we were saying, we said, the three of us including of course Mizuno,

ACTOR 2. Ogawa is like… right, right… For us, like I said, beyond first impressions, in other words, she was actually a healing presence? Like a nurse type? That was the kind of talk we were getting all into… Well in the end, more than anyone else, it was Mizuno for whom that Nightingale image… right, right… landed, your special nurse-like-energy, to sum it up but… or like, I think you probably thought that was a very old-man-joke kind of thing to say but, or more like, that wasn't even really a joke but,

ACTOR 2. But hey, well that's because just now, there was a part of me that said that to be daring, no, really, I mean, because in reality, I am an old man, I'm aware of that, and furthermore, I have to work at being more aware, on many different levels, so that adds to the reason I felt I had to say that to her myself… right, right… uh- then from Ogawa's reaction it was not altogether untrue either, and we were like, Oh, that's how it is, our perception isn't totally off the mark, that's how it was, and that was like for us anyway a shock to be perceived that way…uh- I mean Mizuno is easily an old man… in other words well we were too but… Right, right… But Ogawa says she's like eight years younger, that's, uh, eight years is like, when we hit drinking age, you just got out of elementary school right, is what that means, right? Wow, if you think about it like that, what is the right reaction to have right now, what is the optimum thought to have of all thoughts, so now, nothing from our prior experiences comes to mind that really captures the quandary but, that's the, but, I've got it, Ogawa, right now, putting aside the fact that we're discussing a specific girl named Ogawa, about whom one could say this or that, the idea of a girl who's more than a little younger, in other words, oh, common sense would say oh about two to three years, that's a pretty significant age difference but, uh, the fact that with the girl going out with Mizuno there's even more of a difference, oh, really, she's even younger that that, kind of is the story which generally, inspires or embraces a special, what is it, not envy but, honestly something like that, or not like that but it's a fact, yes,

ACTRESS 1. Ah, yes... I said, "Ah yes" even though there is this feeling that like I shouldn't say "Ah yes" myself but... But it's no, as a way of being told that, ah, yes, yes, this is all stuff I know, obviously, I mean even if I pretended not to know I know, that's the truth, so by saying "ah, yes" it was just that, I thought it would be more honest, and I'm not just being defensive... Of course I could have innocuously NOT said, "Ah yes" but that's just, I don't know, the opposite of knowing or like saying, "Oh I didn't know," kind of, I mean I don't know but, that's all that is, or like, this is just sounding super defensive in the end, but...

ACTOR 1. ...um, about what Kawakami said to Ogawa just now, I am generally in agreement with what he said now, but there is one point on which our opinions subtly differ, which is like, my feeling towards Ogawa right now, or rather, not towards Ogawa, but maybe really towards Mizuno, and that is, if I may, well for instance, if she is, say, hanging around, it seems at first glance, there are all these different issues that come up, as you get to reach a certain age it can't be helped, so anyway, for example... well there's a part of me that feels timid about giving a for example, like it might be bad luck to speak about it because it might come true kind of... in other words, if I were to really go for the jugular, if a woman is more or less around that spoiling age, you might make all sorts of assumptions, not assumptions but...

ACTOR 1. ...There are like so-called transition periods, you might say, but for women in particular, is what I had been feeling these days, and I, men have... or like "for women in particular" is, I just now said "in particular" but that delves into the realm of, then do men in particular NOT have such transition periods? but, it's not that they don't, in particular, I mean men are from the get-go, what do you think Kawakami, don't they not have it, would you say? or like they don't need it really, because there's no physiological limitation, that's what I believe,

ACTOR 1. So Kawakami might seem a little bit deflated just now, I thought, and I don't think there's any reason to be deflated, I'd brought this *(indicating the carton of cigarettes)* as a present for Kawakami, actually, and I gave it to him for his birthday but... kinda like why not smoke like a chimney, go ahead, as if you're going to finish off this whole carton today, in one day,

ACTOR 1. ...there might not even be a line you cross at 30 per se, that's totally, the fact that it looks like there is for a guy is an illusion? On one hand, like the equator or like, I, when I was a kid I believed that the equator was an actual red line, and in the ocean there was a kind of rope like in a swimming pool, pretty much all the way until I was in middle school... Right, but the line at 30 is, no way, there IS no line, it doesn't exist... but women have it? I mean I don't know, man, but, like a physical... so that makes perfect sense right, women have it so men think they do too, the men match the women, or they're dragged into it, or made to match them, that's all there is to it, I mean on a judgment call, women are 100 percent in the wrong about this, am I wrong?

ACTOR 1. So my one phrase reaction to those kinds of women, I mean I say this in front of you because Ogawa, you'll forgive me because you're still 22 years old, but, ...well, shut the hell up! Right?

ACTOR 1. ... But really there's this kind of the standard at
  30, and for Ogawa to have 8 years til then was like, a
  reprieve for Mizuno, and that, for Kato, was the most
  niggling point,

ACTOR 1. How can I put it, once they cross that age bound-
  ary, they focus their laser beams on us, which is total
  pressure, the laser beam emitted from a girl who's at
  that stage is like, wow, I mean totally get off of me! You
  know, but Ogawa, you don't even give off that beam,
  right? How wonderful is that, that you can't even emit,
  really you should treasure that, because that's it, I
  mean the point that makes me envious of Mizuno is,...
  essentially, Ogawa is YOUNG! 22 years old! Which is
  eight years younger, eight years till 30, like, you can
  enjoy the World Cup two more times before she starts
  emitting that beam, Mizuno's situation is like a dream
  come true,

ACTOR 1. ...and having said that much, Kato got swept up
  by his own excitement and after this accidentally... he
  almost blurted out that Mizuno himself was, up until
  very recently, face-to-face with that line like me,

ACTOR 1. ...Mizuno, up until really very recently, had been
  dating a girl for 5 years and they'd just split up, she
  was just a normal, well her personality wasn't bad, kind
  of girl named Maeno, which means "former," who on
  one level, had a very fateful name... but despite the
  break up, he had this huge extreme rebound, and to
  talk about how much of a rebound it was, well, not to
  be like it's this much of a rebound but, really, it was
  such an amazing refreshing rebound wave that Mizuno
  caught... is what I almost let myself accidentally say in
  front of Ogawa, which might have been on Ogawa's
  end, like What? kind of possibility... but I now think,
  though this might be overly optimistic, but, that I was
  just borderline safe but

ACTRESS 1. ...but Ogawa had picked up on this because,
  the atmosphere was like, well, full of it.... well, but
  even for Ogawa, if she had been asked, if she could

possibly have thought that Mizuno had never had a girlfriend before her, she'd have to admit, uh, well, that she may have thought that, that's what she'd probably have to answer but,

ACT TWO: CONTINUATION

ACTRESS 1. So next is the second act, and here, two other part-timers come in, they were named Shimizu and Takeuchi, and they were both a touch younger than Kato and Kawakami, and the two of them came in about a certain matter,

*(**ACTORS** 3 and 4 enter.)*

ACTOR 3. Um, Kato, or Kawakami, if one of you, it doesn't matter who, usually I ask Mizuno to do this but, when Mizuno's not here, like right now, I guess more often I've asked Kato to help out with this a few times, so in that sense, I'm asking again, but for my part it doesn't really matter who, as long as it's taken care of... Um so there's approximately one guy who's just come into the store, one of those Jesus-types, that needs to be taken care of I mean doesn't it stink in here? Or has it not reached back here yet? So, um, Kato, I'm sorry, but can you please take care of it? Kato, Ok thanks,

*(**ACTOR 3** exits.)*

*(**ACTOR 1** exits.)*

ACTOR 4. So the main topic of Act Two is Kawakami, and for Kawakami, he wasn't quite finished with his conversation with Ogawa from Act One, about the details of how specifically her relationship with Mizuno developed... or in other words, um, how did it all unfold, like what were the initial exchanges, or like, when did this all begin in the first place, or in other words, "was there like a definitive moment in which those feelings towards him were born," or like "so what's it like right now, are you guys still in the honeymoon phase?" These were some of the questions that, I mean we haven't gotten deep enough to ask and want to ask but, but Ogawa don't you actually want to talk about it? You do, don't you? Or am I way off the mark?

ACTRESS 1. …Oh, sure, totally, I do want to talk about it so, ask away,

ACTOR 4. Oh really?

ACTRESS 1. Yes,

ACTOR 4. …Huh, but so Ogawa you say you're eight years younger than him, right? Eight years is –

ACTRESS 1. Yes,

ACTOR 4. That means when we hit drinking age, you were just getting out of elementary school, whoah when you think about it that way, wow, a girl your age must think we're like old men, I mean that's what I'd think, and to tell you the truth, that realization just suddenly struck me like, boom, just a second ago, like a thunderbolt!

ACTOR 4. …although it wasn't a complete surprise that such a realization would dawn on me, because to be honest, and this is totally a personal thing, but it had been a pretty eventful day already

ACTOR 4. …it was sinking in,

ACTOR 2. …Right, right.

ACTOR 4. That's what Kawakami was thinking in that moment,

ACTOR 2. …Right, right…. or like, that it was an event-ful day, is kind of an opaque way to put it, because he wasn't like really that close to her so… and that probably is connected too, whether consciously or unconsciously… But seriously, even putting aside any consideration or comparing myself to Ogawa, there was definitely already a real like consciousness of "oh, I'm an old man" that kind of awareness, it wasn't like something that came about out of the blue today of all days, to tell you the truth… right, right… but truthfully, it was internally, like as if a thunderbolt had skewered all of my internal organs in one flash, I was gripped by this kind of terror. And to be honest, it was the first time I really felt that way in my whole life…

Right, right, gripped by terror... I just couldn't be all like, "Yeah, so that's the deal, today is my birthday and I have at last crossed the threshold into my 30s," or like, "yeah dude, I'm seriously like freaked out man," I mean I wasn't going to be able to play it off like a joke today, I'm sorry, but

ACTOR 2. ...Yeah, it's that, it hasn't really sunk in for real, the fact that I'm 30, or like, to be honest, yeah, honestly I am panicked, or it's not just that I'm panicked but... this might sound like an excuse but, people might be all like, "What are you, an idiot? Get real already, look reality in the eye, and you know, blah blah blah"... and I would have no line of defense ready... but whatever, but, that's not it, I mean it is that but, I am panicked about turning 30 but it's not as simple as that, or like, I actually have turned 30, but to be honest it really hasn't hit me at all, it's like I'm completely deluding myself... and that's where I look at myself and I'm like, wait, is this OK? And like, of course it's not OK, and that's where the panic comes in... because I'm like NOT really panicked at all... when in fact at this stage, and by this stage I mean, say the end is the edge of a cliff, and I'm just a scant two or three steps away from that edge, easily, so like shouldn't I perhaps be more panicked? And yet nevertheless, I'm only a little bit panicked, and that's why I think I'm totally screwed up... I mean, is this OK? I mean wouldn't a normal guy who found himself in this predicament like have the thought of wanting to kill himself? ...Right, right... I mean having one or two thoughts like that is normal I think, it's not going to put a curse on you, so you see I am perfectly aware that that kind of mindset exists, of course... but understand that that doesn't mean that I actually have those thoughts, or that I am feeling that kind of pressure, it's just that the idea that the world creates that kind of pressure, and that's normal... and it's not like I'm judging that pressure either, here, in fact it's quite the opposite, I understand it, totally, like yeah, I've been raised and fed for all these years and now look at me, what the heck am I doing with my life, that's the state we're in, and even looking ahead, no matter how you look at the forecast, there's a slim to none chance of any drastic upward swing on the horizon, in fact I'd say that with 100% certainty, so that's why here I am, doing this… um, in anticipation of impending misfortune, I'm preparing lots of… right, right… I'm going to try to include plenty of portentous phrases from here, because I am making this video to function as a kind of video will, so that even if people who didn't know that watched it, they wouldn't be like what the hell is this and not get it, I want to be careful about that, so from here on out I'd like to try to make this video little by little, easier to understand on that level.

ACTOR 2. …But, …right, right, …I took this opportunity to think about when or rather where I turned to become like this, looking back at the exactly 30 years I've been alive like a movie, I might have been what you'd call, what I was talking about earlier, I think that it's necessary for human beings to have experiences while they're still young, that force them into a real panic, or like, I'm sorry, I don't actually believe what I just said at all, it's like something someone like a commentator would say or like something you'd read, or saw on TV, and to be able to say it yourself, I mean, I'm not sure whether I agree with it or not… only, in this situation, I would have to say that nothing of that sort ever happened to me, or like, yeah…

ACTOR 2. …But, so where are you supposed to have had an experience like that? Or rather, you can have experiences like that but in like an establishment? I mean, literally an institution? Like a regular company? Hmmm, but if I were to answer that, it would be the most predictable, boring story… Or like OK, so I've come this far in life without even an episode like one of those hazing processes that upper class men put the freshman through in middle or high school, in the boys dorm, like, "get over here," and, "all right strip off your clothes," and then, "yes, sir," and like, "What the hell are you doing take off you shorts too," and like, "are you serious?" "Damn right I'm serious" "Yes sir," and like, "OK so now that you're butt naked, let's see you do something in front of us, something, like some joke that uses your full nudity to its maximum potential." "Oh, yes sir, then… I'm a helicopter," like an important life experience of that kind of magnitude and process, I have gone without, and I am the one who understands best what I've missed in life, like shut up, I know that I've come this far without it and ultimately that's why, here I am… making this video will, by myself, so, so now, so what?

ACTOR 2. …And that story just made me think, like what would happen if I got totally naked in my video will? … Maybe it would be like super hysterical? Or like would it be the opposite, like make people cry, I wonder… I'm not going to do that, because it's not my intention to make people cry, and I don't actually want to get naked either, and whether people would find it funny or pitiful, in any case the first reaction would be revulsion anyway…

ACTOR 2. …But on the other hand, if it does just turn people off, that might actually be good, I mean if you were to see a video of a friend of yours, who was talking into the camera butt naked, well I guess there's the question of whether you'd watch it at all in the first place, because the first reaction would be revulsion, not compassion, normally… hmm, maybe it would be better to take it that far, I don't know but, I wonder if it would be good, I wonder…

(He exits.)

*(**ACTOR 3** re-enters.)*

ACTOR 4. The reason the two of us felt like we had the right to just demand Kato to do what we asked him to do before was because our comic book cafe is in the middle of Shinjuku and because such a variety of people come here, in both type and in numbers, and among our varied customers, there are people who are like are you really a customer, or, in fact they aren't actually customers… we've been referring to one of these kinds of people as the Jesus-types and they're these people who are living in the great outdoors, even here in the midst of the Shinjuku urban center, and once in a while they try to come inside here… One particular regular, this old man whose face is totally cracked open, he comes in acting all entitled and asking for a "five-hour pack"… It's like no, no, man your face is all cracked open, obviously you've been sleeping outside, and I totally accept your situation, I mean, it's fine with me if you come here to sleep, but we've got standards you know, I mean just look at yourself, kind of –

ACTOR 3. …Also the smell, or like, it's just too unbearable… I mean I'm not like the department of sanitation or anything but

ACTOR 4. Yeah totally, or like, when you look at their hands, their fingernails are completely black, and after you've seen it with your own eyes, it's like, hey, mister, what do you expect, I'm sorry, I can't let you into the store, and that's something on our side that can be assessed in just a few seconds, but also, on our side, the whole interaction is kind of sad, and there's this feeling of wanting to at least go through the motions of think-ing about it to prolong the time necessary to reach the inevitable conclusion, I guess you could call it a kind of sympathy

ACTOR 3. …This kind of thing was something that we talked about before… And it was pretty sudden, right… Mizuno happened to be there when we were talking and he was listening to us, and then all of a sudden, he just completely lost his shit… we were like, Huh? but he was kind of like, don't you have any sense of basic human decency towards your fellow man?! kind of thing

ACTOR 4. …Yeah he was out of control. I mean I totally understand how some people might lose their shit, but for Mizuno to lose his shit like that so suddenly was… a bit questionable… I mean, you're free to lose your shit, but if you're going to lose your shit, there is something like, "your right to lose it," is that weird… I mean, from our perspective, sorry to be gross but, these dudes, they smell bad, yeah, but it's like, hm, isn't that the smell of alcohol mixed in with that terrible stink? You know,

ACTOR 4. But it wasn't like we were saying the rudest possible things to these guys either, and I want to be clear about that, we spoke to them in a tactful tone of voice, and very politely, I mean we do that now, it wasn't always like that but

ACTOR 3. Mizuno chewed us out about that once before… and at that time we accepted what he said pretty obediently, and since then we've been very polite to them consistently, and that's pretty honorable of us, if you think about it… but in terms of everything else, Mizuno is a hypocrite, I mean he totally drinks whatever he wants in the cafe, and it was only this thing about the homeless guys that he took so seriously, and recently we started to realize that Mizuno was the type of guy who had pretty uneven standards,

ACTOR 3. …So if Mizuno is gonna go that berserk over this, then from our point of view,

ACTOR 4. Yeah totally,

ACTOR 3. Then let's give him real reason to go berserk, you know, from now on, everything with the stinky old guys should be handled by Mizuno, no matter who the shift manager is at the front counter, we'll go out of our way and get Mizuno to handle it, at least, because I mean the way he lost it that one time was pretty crazy, like is

he himself aware of it? And we really didn't deserve it
you know and he's got to earn that right to blow his
top, am I wrong?

ACTOR 3. …there was that and the other thing we decided
was that of course there would be times when Mizuno
wouldn't be on shift, so in that event what should
happen is, we'll get Kawakami or Kato to take care of
it, that was the upshot of it, it had to go that far, for us
to feel it was fair… that's what we thought,

ACTOR 4. …Um, and the reason the names of Kato and
Kawakami are being brought up here is that the three
of them were like a package deal, at our comic book
cafe, the three of them were the only, um, I'm sorry
everyone, they were all over 30, which was over the
hill from me and Takeuchi's point of view… On our
side, what we've been calling that trio behind their
back was… I mean we on the young side are only just
26 or 27 but, … to talk about the three of them, we'd
taken the first syllable of each of their three names
"Mi" from Mizuno, "Ka" from Kato, and another "Ka"
from Kawakami, and together referred to that trio as
"MiKaKa," it doesn't have any deeper meaning, but
that was their group name that we used to talk about
them secretly,

ACTOR 3. So basically we decided that if Mizuno were going
to freak out to that extent, then MiKaKa altogether
should shoulder the responsibility for taking care of all
of those Jesus-types, but… we seriously thought about
going straight to Mizuno with this idea, but there was
a part of us that knew that this idea itself was pretty
crazy, so we thought we'd first bring this to the store
manager and discuss it with him, so yeah, that's what
we did, we went to discuss it,

ACTOR 3. …then what the Store Manager said was like, OK
I understand, he said, I will, and this is the manager
talking, I will create a manual that details the best
ways to handle those kinds of people, it'll be a manual
just for such a situation, that's what we'll do, and let's

handle these people according to the manual, so that's what happened, but because we were all part-timers and we couldn't memorize very detailed rules, everything had to be simple enough for a monkey to memorize… and ultimately, as the solution for how to handle the situation, it basically boiled down to, without exception, just don't let them inside, and seriously it had to be that straightforward because otherwise none of the employees were going to remember,

ACTOR 3. …and so it was like go ahead and invoke the store manager as much as you like, in other words, if one of those men who you refer to as a Jesus-type comes in, just tell them that the store manager has strictly forbidden you to allow them inside, and that you're just a part-timer, and there's nothing you can do so you're sorry, all in one breath, and if he still doesn't leave, tell him straight-up that you're going to call the cops, and that's not an empty threat, you can just go ahead and call the cops, even if the cops tell you not to call them each time over such a small thing, and they bitch about it, don't worry about it, because they actually don't get too snarky these days, so call away, is what he said,

ACTOR 4. That's what we were told by the store manager,

ACTOR 3. Yup

ACTOR 4. But it's still a pain for us to deal with them at all, and so in the end we get MiKaKa to deal with them, or we make Mizuno deal with them, because Mizuno said himself that that was fine,

(**ACTOR 1** *enters.*)

ACTOR 4. …So that's why earlier I came in to ask Kato to deal with a Jesus, and now Kato comes back in, and I was like, thanks for dealing with Jesus, but when I saw Kato, his mood was totally different

ACTOR 1. *(taking mop in hand)* It's really turned out strangely… The old man for some reason had some money with him, a 1000 yen bill, and I was thinking like, whoah, and I let him pull it out and whoah, I let him pay, I thought, and I was like no no we can't let you come in, ...and he said, "Huh, what are you talking about?" and, "What are you talking about, I've got the dough, what's the problem" he said, *(laughing)* I was thinking problem?!, like, "uh and where exactly did you get this money?" and he said, "What the hell are you talking about, I worked for it just like anybody else, money is money, you can't be prejudiced against me," and I was like no, no, no, and he was like on and on and on, and I was like man come on don't go apeshit on me, but he did, all of a sudden, and those kinds of people, all of a sudden, they go crazy and get crazy violent, and you can't understand a word they're saying, and you have no idea what they're gonna try to do... so before it gets out of hand, I thought I'd preempt him and, you know, take him out... and well, he just ran out of the store, but he did leave a trail of blood on the floor, so I thought I'd better wipe that up so the customers aren't freaked out by it.

(He exits.)

ACTRESS 1. By the way, Ogawa, in the end, wasn't able to talk about her love life in more detail at all... anyway that's the end of Act Two,

ACT THREE: THE LOVERS' ROOM

(**ACTRESS 2** *and* **ACTRESS 3** *enter*)

ACTRESS 2. A certain woman *(indicating **ACTRESS 3**)*… This woman, who is just like a temp, normally, for work, but… but this isn't about work, actually, we're just going to delve into her private life now, at the beginning of Act Three… This woman has had a boyfriend for a pretty long time… well, it's not "has had," anymore, but "had," …and anyway recently the person who is now her ex-boyfriend sent her this awful e-mail,

ACTRESS 3. Well at that point, he wasn't officially an ex yet, …but the situation between them had gotten pretty weird already…

ACTRESS 2. …you could pretty much say that this e-mail was like the precise reason or like cause for her to make that clear decision inside that OK it's time to get rid of this guy, it was that awful…

ACTRESS 3. But it wasn't the e-mail, in the end he came to her house… I mean first it was the e-mail… and the e-mail… it was like, "can I come over right now" and it was super late at night, and totally out of the blue, in fact it was almost midnight by that point already… but he was like there's something I need to talk to you about or discuss, right now… it may have been closer to one o'clock, I mean she could have been asleep, ordinarily, what if she had been asleep… I guess if she hadn't replied he probably would have just given up for that moment… but the girl wrote back that it would be OK… so he came over,

ACTRESS 3. …So then, the guy starts talking about… and listening to him, it was… in the middle of it, I mean not even in the middle but pretty soon after he started,

I was like, what? This is what he wants to discuss? At his age, that's what he's worried about, Jesus! Like, who cares?

ACTRESS 3. ...or like probably by this point, it was more that she didn't have any feelings for him anymore, than the actual subject of what he was talking about, that things turned out this way I think, but now we're going to do the part about what this woman heard that night, and that conversation,

ACTRESS 3. ...I was talking to my friend about the conversation... and I had been thinking for a long time before that I had to dump him I had to dump him, and my friend was like, "You're so right, you have to break up with him, he is awful, I think, especially after hearing this story... it's like what? This guy should just roll over and die, I mean he is totally in the wrong, no matter how objectively you look at it," and we were just going to catch the subway together when she said that after I'd told her the story...

ACTRESS 3. ...But that was not the only reason, it wasn't like that pushed her over the edge, to the point of no return and she broke up with him that night... there were a lot of different things that had built up over time...but I do think that night was definitely a turning point,

ACTRESS 3. ...When I got his e-mail, I was like you know, I have to get up in the morning to go to work, but I replied to him, "OK, you can come over" and then he was like, "OK, I'm coming over now" and he showed up pretty quickly,

ACTRESS 3. ..."I picked up some beer at the 7-Eleven" he said, "I even got us two" like... was this an obligatory beer? Or some kind of gift? And when I looked at the can, it wasn't even real beer, it wasn't even like a wine cooler, it was some crappy third-rate beer, three percent.

ACTRESS 3. ...So he started talking about why he was feeling depressed, and the whole story of what got him so depressed was just so pathetic,

ACTRESS 3. "I went into work like normal for my shift, and a customer came in, dressed in a suit, like an office worker, and I'm pretty sure it was a guy I knew from grade school" he said, and

ACTRESS 3. "I'm positive it was him, that face of his... he lived in my neighborhood, and we were in the same grade in elementary school... I'm pretty sure it was him... if I imagine his face from back then and how it might naturally get bigger and older, it would be that face, the face of the guy who came into the cafe today and I was like... Huh? Maybe that's him, I thought... I knew I recognized him from somewhere, I thought... I say recognize, but I wasn't managing the front counter at that moment, in fact I was cleaning up around the drink dispensers so it wasn't like I came face to face with him, in fact he probably didn't even see me... I was watching him from a distance, like that girl from "Star of the Giants"*, just kind of glancing in the direction of the counter,"

ACTRESS 3. "...Of course it'd been 20 years, well not 20, but so I can't be 100% sure at all, but... but still, I'm pretty sure it was him."

ACTRESS 2. ...Uh-huh... What? And that was what got him depressed?

ACTRESS 3. "Yeah"

ACTRESS 2. Oh, really,

(Pause)

ACTRESS 3. ...at that moment, the thing I was in charge of was... we call it drink duty but... If you've been to a comic book cafe, I think you'd know what I was talking about but, there's a free drink corner where there are these machines that the customers can use to serve themselves, you know, drink dispensers, so I was on drink duty and checking on fluid levels, like replacing any coffee powder if it had run out, and like wiping up the counter if customers had spilt anything, so I was supervising that area... when I noticed the guy at the

---

*Translator's note: Dramatic manga about baseball which inspired an anime TV show.

front of the line at the counter, and I was like, wait is that Atsushi?…The guy was wearing like a normal suit, so before I was like he looks just like Atsushi, he was just an ordinary like "one of them" salaryman, that's all I thought,… our kind of establishment is for, you know, people just killing time between appointments, or just wanting to play hooky for a second, that's the best use of our place I think, we're in Shinjuku too, so,

ACTRESS 3. So I assumed he was one of those guys at first, but then I was like, wait, maybe I know this guy?… Could I really recognize someone after not seeing them for 20 years, and him wearing a suit and all? And just from catching a glimpse of them randomly in Shinjuku? What was making me so aware of him? If I hadn't thought of someone for nearly 20 years, but I'm still able to recall his face, where, and how was that memory stored, for so long? I thought….

ACTRESS 3. And then we made eye contact, for about two seconds maybe one and a half seconds, an awkward length of time to make eye contact, I think maybe we both felt it, a length of time that makes you aware of it, so that's what makes me think that he really was Atsushi? I'm still wondering about it… I mean I say one and a half seconds but really it's not like I had timed it but it was just how long it felt,

ACTRESS 3. …the house that Atsushi lived in was really close to mine when we were kids… he was on the next block… I grew up in Kanagawa, and… we actually played together a lot in grade school, our parents were in some neighborhood group together as I recall, and that's how we got to know each other since before kindergarten…. but from middle school, because I went to a private school for middle and high school, we stopped hanging out so much, because he went on to public school like most kids…

ACTRESS 3. …In grade school for Golden Week*, our families would take vacations together to Hakone and stuff, or summer vacations to the beach in Izu, that's how

---

*Translator's note: National week-long holiday.

close we were… we even went skiing together in the winter, just once, over winter vacation…

ACTRESS 3. …I have a vague memory of once going to some quiet place, where was it, it was definitely not Naeba or anywhere lively like that, it was more of a subdued, family vacation type place

(Pause. **ACTOR 5** *enters.)*

ACTOR 5. …But if Mizuno had asked Atsushi… where was it that we went skiing that time? Atsushi would have replied, "That must have been Gunma or Takahara, I believe" that much he would have remembered from seeing some sightseeing pamphlet and the name of Gunma having been burned into his memory…

ACTRESS 3. …But when you think about it now, that implies that… going on a vacation together with another family…is like they must have been in the same economic class, or like… I mean you never think about that as kids of course but,

ACTRESS 3. …But so when I saw Atsushi at that moment… oh he was wearing like a regular… I mean he's wearing a nice suit, he's probably, you know, compared to me, I thought… getting bonuses at work and stuff,

(pause)

ACTOR 5. …No but really, to tell you the truth… As far as bonuses go… yeah we have them, but they're really pathetic, like practically nonexistent, I mean some bad years, um, you could blow the entire thing going to a chintzy strip club once, I mean that amount of money, isn't it illegal to call that a bonus? Like –

ACTRESS 3. Wha– but at least you get a bonus… or like, I think that's admirable, it's not about the amount of money, but that you get a bonus at all, that means you're that much more legit,

ACTOR 5. No, no no, getting a bonus is not like the Olympics

ACTRESS 3. … Wha– But your bonuses now are pretty good, right?

ACTRESS 3. …I mean I couldn't talk to him like that, because I just wasn't sure, and even if it was him, then what… I wouldn't have known what to say to him, so for both reasons,

ACTRESS 3. But when our eyes met, I feel like he was also like, huh?

(pause)

ACTOR 5. …Or like, to be honest, the moment our eyes met for like two or three seconds, I recognized him pretty immediately… but, inside, I was pretty surprised and I was also afraid if I was mistaken, so I didn't speak to him… and anyway what would we say to each other? I never suspected anything like this would happen all of a sudden, at a comic book cafe,

ACTOR 5. I'm actually a pretty frequent user of comic book cafes, but I rarely come to Shinjuku for work, and that day it just so happened I had to meet with my first client in West Shinjuku, and after that I had some extra time til lunch, so as I was walking back towards the station, through the blocks of high-rise buildings, because I had the time, and as I was walking I was of course thinking about what to get for lunch and at first I was looking for a good ramen place, but as I was look- ing, I started to think that maybe ramen wasn't what I needed today, because I'd gone out drinking last night and my stomach wasn't feeling so hot so I didn't feel like ramen, so why was I looking for a ramen place to begin with, but anyway I thought maybe I didn't need such a heavy lunch, plus I was hoping to squeeze in a power nap too… because actually I hadn't really slept or bathed last night so,

ACTOR 5. …So I go to those comic book cafes pretty fre- quently, whenever I feel a little tired, or if I want to take a nap, because they usually have showers and they have all sorts of snacks to eat – that day I did end up eating instant ramen and a rice ball, I know, if I was going to eat ramen after all, I should have gone to some famous ramen joint written up in the magazines but –

ACTOR 5. …I thought I'd find a place easily if I just walked around Shinjuku, I'm talking about a comic book cafe, not ramen place… But, comic book cafe or not, I wasn't in the habit of coming to Shinjuku much at all, so I don't know it very well, I mean if it had been Ikebukuro, I would have known where to go, in fact I could probably draw a map of all the comic book cafes in the area, but… I was able to find one pretty quick, it was Shinjuku after all – and the main thing in the building where the comic book cafe was a kara-oke place, but the upper floors of the building were this comic book cafe… so I got on the elevator and went up… and I got off the elevator and the guy at the counter said, "Welcome" or something, and did I "want to use the internet?" "Oh, yes." "Then please use booth number whatever, and you can settle the bill when you leave and blah blah blah" kind of thing,

ACTOR 5. …then that was what I was doing when Mizuno was watching me… and that night Mizuno went to this woman Maeno's house after work, he went to her apartment to tell her about running into me, appar-ently,

(pause)

ACTRESS 3. …right… that was right around lunch time but– …I had to work til 10 pm… I had a long shift again, today…

ACTRESS 3. …and the whole rest of the day, I kinda felt depressed… I mean I don't really understand why I feel like this but,

ACTRESS 3. …But recently, I've been trying to think, ratio-nally… like our parents… I mean they paid for my college education, in my case for me AND my sister, I mean that's actually pretty amazing, don't you think?

ACTRESS 2. Yeah, amazing

ACTRESS 3. Yeah… or don't you think it's amazing?

ACTRESS 2. Or like, amazing? I've always thought it was amazing,

ACTRESS 3. Yeah… or, I mean everybody's parents, right? That's the norm, so, maybe it's not amazing?

ACTRESS 2. Or like, it's not really about quantity, right? Even if a lot of people do it, it doesn't change the fact that it's still amazing, it's not any less amazing just because more people do it, I mean I really feel that way towards my parents, I've felt that way since like high school and stuff,

ACTRESS 3. Oh, yeah… Are you like mad? At me?

ACTRESS 3. Because I have a reason to feel depressed right now, and I'm saying I'm depressed, I'm depressed, is that what you're mad about? *(laughing)* … You're mad at me right now, right?

ACTRESS 2. Or like… Shinjuku is a particularly high traffic area, and as far as a comic book cafe I'm sure the chances of people going there is pretty high… You've been working there for over five years… and millions of people go through Shinjuku station everyday, so I don't think it's particularly shocking for you to run into someone you know, in fact it's almost strange that it hadn't happened before, I think,

ACTRESS 2. …Or rather, also, but… um like he's depressed, right, or so he says… but this is what he's getting depressed over, at this point in his life, after all this time, that's what I was thinking,… I mean, "Today when I went into my shift I ran into a like childhood acquaintance at lunch time" he says… So what? Isn't it too late for you to be feeling like depressed about your life? Like really!… Why didn't you just say hello to him like a normal person… Depressed, he says… Um, well, then if you're going to be that pathetic… I mean, it's really disgusting, you're 30 years old and your life is over!

ACTRESS 2. …or like, even the fact that he was able to say to me "I'm depressed" without any hesitation… It's the absolute worst thing for me to hear, and to not understand that, it's amazing, he really doesn't get it, it's really not normal, I mean even before then, but, it was shocking to think that he was this dense,

ACTRESS 2. Hey do you have any idea what I'm mulling over and being a big poo about?

(pause)

ACTRESS 3. But… thinking back on it now… he was actually having the exact opposite reaction thinking that it was a real coincidence for him to have run into someone like that in a place like Shinjuku… in retrospect, I think that I could have been a little more thoughtful… that you'd run into someone because you're in Shinjuku, that logic is sounds, but just because it's correct, I kind of pushed it on him, almost aggressively… I mean the logic itself that I was insisting on, might have been correct, but what he was thinking, that conversely, it was rare to run into someone you knew in Shinjuku, I understand that thinking, in fact I understood it then, in fact I knew from the beginning that that's what he was thinking, mean I knew he felt that way from the beginning…

ACTRESS 3. …there was definitely room for sympathy, and points of understanding, I thought….. because well he was a part-timer… barely scraping by… but of course, I myself,… I'm a temp… and a temp, is really just the same thing, just a different word,

(pause)

ACTRESS 2. Hey, do you have any idea what I'm mulling over and being a big poo about?

ACTRESS 2. … feeling sorry for yourself is… Go ahead, feel sorry for yourself all you want, is what I think, but when you go vomiting that on me, when it becomes a problem that affects me… uh- if it's that bad, don't just mope around, go and DO something.

ACTRESS 3. …I mean truly, why do I even have to say this out loud, is this the role I have to play, to say things like that? I would hope that you'd been told this kind of thing by someone else, a long time ago, or like you have, right? And it just didn't really impact you, right? Or like, come on… how old do you think you are, anyway?

ACTRESS 2. ...Can't you understand that I've had it up to here? You think this is completely out of the blue? I bet you actually think I'm in the wrong for losing my temper like this... It's my bad for having unreasonable expectations?

ACTRESS 2. ...Maybe that's true... I mean... I have really exercised my patience, I mean I don't want to put it like that, but really... I'm impressed that I've been able to be so tolerant with someone like you, but enough is enough, I can't anymore, life is...

ACTOR 5. Someone like me?

ACTRESS 2. ...When I realized that there was no need for me to pity him over nothing, or play the martyr anymore, I was like phew! so relieved... I mean it may sound rude to say "someone like you"... but there's no other way to put it... I mean if I were to wait, or continue being patient with him... I mean it would be never-ending... and I think it's on one level a kind of self-pity for me to wait so long for nothing... it would just drag on and on, so that's why I decided to cut it off... but to do that, I thought I had treat him like "someone like that"... and not just think that but really,

(pause)

ACTOR 5. ...In Act One, as it was explained, it probably seemed like Maeno's age was kind of the reason that Mizuno ended it with her, but in truth it was actually Maeno who dumped Mizuno, you see,

ACTOR 5. ...When she broke up with him she said some pretty nasty things to him like, "Don't you think it's a little late to be getting depressed over something like that?" and like, "maybe you should just die" and like

ACTOR 5. ...That was the first and last time anyone's said anything like that to him... "maybe you should just die, take this opportunity... maybe that's what's best for you yourself? ...I think that maybe you have no reason to keep on living, I mean what are you living for? That's what I want to ask... I mean you're 30 and still living like this, it's too late to even be thinking about what a state you're in..."

ACTOR 5. ...and to hear this from me, is it like OW, stab? But watching you, it really makes me want to say that to you... it's actually amazing that you keep living in a normal psychological state in your situation,

ACTOR 5. ...I don't think I ever told you to be more manly... I don't want to have to say things like that... but ... for the first time in my life, I feel like maybe I owe it to you to say it because I still do have some feelings for you... wow, and I'm feeling like, hey you really are a good guy... and really we ought to remember this moment, because it was the first time I felt like I should say something that before I didn't ever want to have to say to anyone... and I really mean it, this is a record for me...

ACTOR 5. That's what she said to me, nag nag nag for a long time, on and on... I mean to say to someone, "why don't you just die," is like who the hell do you think you are, what right does this woman think she have to say stuff like this...

ACTOR 5. ...Or like, I KNOW all this, all of it, I know that's what she thinks of me, that that's how I seem, like "Oh, this is the kind of guy who is ruining the future of Japan, these guys who have no income, who aren't married, who can't pay their taxes or social security who are total slackers" or like "how old does he think he is, working in a place like this, what the hell is he thinking at his age" kind of, I feel that gaze on me, you don't have to tell me...

ACTOR 5. ...It's like all right, shut up

ACTOR 5. ...and what pisses me off even more is that air of "oh yes yes, I understand where you're coming from" like that attitude that they are different from us, because they've got their own philosophy and view of life, so it doesn't matter what we say to them because we just have totally different values, that whole air of,

ACTRESS 2. ...Huh, if you want to shut them up, why don't you say it out loud, if that's what you're thinking

ACTRESS 2. ...I mean you just have it in your head that everyone is looking at you that way, like so dead-end, so over... But you shouldn't assume that's what they're thinking, that's what I think... I mean you are making it up, right, out of self-pity, that people think those things of you? That's all I'm saying, aren't those two different things?

ACTOR 5. No, no, no that is what people think of me for sure, I'm not just making it up

ACTRESS 2. Who's people?

ACTOR 5. No, no, no... I know what you're trying to say...

ACTRESS 2. No, who's people? I mean has anyone specific ever told you that to your face?

(pause)

ACTOR 5. ...I mean, when you said, "Aren't those two different things" OK, they might be on a hypothetical level, they might be hypothetically different, but in reality they're the same,

ACTOR 5. ... it's, really idealistic, maybe, I mean this hypothetical might be too difficult to dissect but... I mean in actuality, there's no way, it's too difficult to distinguish the two, except on a hypothetical level right,

(pause)

ACTRESS 2. Has anyone specific ever told you that to your face?

ACTOR 5. ...No,

ACTRESS 2. So when you say you just perceive that attitude towards you... from the world, you're just assuming that people are saying that about you, right?

ACTOR 5. Right, right,

(pause)

ACTRESS 2. ...The fact that you act as if someone has said something like that to your face, when nobody actually has... and to take those presumptions so far... I mean, wouldn't you think that's a bit, you know,

ACTOR 5. ...Uh-uh, I don't think so... what do you mean, "you know"?

ACTRESS 2. ...you may think it's humility or a safety net or like a defense mechanism... but I think that actually you're mistaken in your thinking, I think you just feel sorry for yourself,

(pause)

ACTRESS 2. ...Why do you force yourself to feel all this pressure, when nobody's actually said anything like that to you? I mean, doesn't it piss you off? Why doesn't it piss you off and make you want to fight back?

ACTRESS 2. ...Or like, that's what I'd hoped you'd do... even if you didn't actually have it in you to fight back, even just to pretend to fight back would have made me feel less contempt... like there might have been some other alternative...

(pause)

ACTOR 5. ...No, no, no... there are plenty of people in the world who HAVE been told that to their face... so what you said before, that it was just my presumptions, it's not, it's not presumption, but then if you were to ask me if I'd been told to my face, I'd have to say no...

ACTOR 5. ...But that might just be an issue about my personality,

(Pause)

ACTRESS 2. ...yeah... so... then why is it that you feel the way someone might feel if they'd been told that they were a pathetic loser, when nobody's said anything like that to your face? Don't you think that's presumptuous? I mean, how can you live an enjoyable life at all from day to day if you feel that way?

ACTRESS 2. ...That's what... being with you, I wish you could put yourself in my shoes, there's that, but even more important is that for yourself... I mean for one thing, isn't it painful to live that way?

(pause)

ACTOR 5. …Uh, I can't believe you just said that that way –
"isn't it painful?" you ask…

ACTRESS 2. Yeah… so… Well, you don't understand at all,
do you,

ACTRESS 2. …When he said, "I can't believe you said that,"
if he had even for one moment before considered,
but ultimately, he just had absolutely no awareness of
how his actions might affect me, like how he might be
the victimizer, so I knew this conversation was going
nowhere… All he can talk about is himself,

(pause)

ACTOR 5. …I mean, yeah, it is painful,

ACTOR 5. …It would be rational to think that if I kept going
like this, I would naturally become homeless, just like,
I would, because, think about it, if my parents, see, naturally they'll die before me, and when you think about
the house and stuff… it's not like I haven't thought
about it, I mean even I can imagine that much,

ACTOR 5. …Of course some people don't have the imagi-
nation, hard to believe, but… you can tell right away
from their attitudes, at the counter… sometimes these
guys come to the store, I guess they really want to rest
in an enclosed space once in a while… or maybe they
really want to read comics, I dunno… they want to be
inside a real building with real walls? …But anyway
they come inside, and they just, because our customers
pay for everything when they leave, they take advan-
tage of us like, they've already smoked our cigarettes,
they've taken a shower, and when they get to the
cashiers and they have no money, it's like what can you
do, they've already used the facilities, like oh well, they
win… Usually you can tell right away with these people
so I refuse to let them in but yeah, I mean… I turn
them away, but I think there are proper ways to turn
them away, you know… but some people they don't
get it, the basic level of decency when dealing with
another human being, and I think they must be idiots,
because they can't connect, they can't imagine…

ACTOR 5. ...So the way I think... If some day I were to become one of these guys... yeah... if I do, maybe, it won't be as bad as I think it is in actuality... Like by that time, there'll probably be lots of guys like me, I mean think about it, definitely more than now, I really think there will be way more people like them, and then, well, I have this weirdly optimistic view too that it may not be such a tragedy, I mean we'll be all right, so... yeah,

(pause)

ACTOR 5. If the air, or like the existence of a mood were definitely a real thing, like for example a ghost, not just a feeling but a real existence,

ACTOR 5. ...that air of: Why don't you fellas get a real job huh, try to land a job? ...I mean if you really put your life on the line, in Japan today, sure it might be difficult, but you should be able to get a job, right, if you get fight for you life... hmmmm... I mean all you guys are college grads, right, so why don't you have the balls to really go after something even once, hmmmm, I mean that's something that's hard for us to understand, right... but maybe it's this... since you fellas have your own unique worldview and philosophy... hmmmm...well, that ought to be respected... hmmmm,

ACTOR 5. ...But see... say for instance I say since you have such a unique worldview and philosophy, let me get you this job, or let me teach you a lot of things about the world, well, you'd say, "Leave me alone" is...but I have to say, even though you're probably thinking "I'm not doing anything bad" that kind of attitude is to a great extent, what is affecting our society, and creating this sense of uncertainty, socially, and I just think they ought to feel some responsibility for that,

ACTOR 5. ...That's how I think Mizuno imagines the people around him talking about him all the time...back in the day, he and I used to play together, and well, that's

ancient history, and anyway I really have no idea what
he is like right now, … so that's why in the end I didn't
talk to him, I spent an hour in the cafe and then left…
I probably won't ever come to this comic book cafe
again, even if I have business in Shinjuku…

(He exits.)

ACT FOUR: INSIDE SHINJUKU STATION

(**ACTRESS 1** *and* **ACTOR 3** *are embracing each other [but at this point, it would be better if this is not totally clear]* **ACTRESS 4** *and* **ACTOR 4** *enter.* **ACTRESS 4** *has a stuffed bear [a Rilakkuma])*

ACTRESS 4. At the station, when it's close to the last train of the night... or sometimes it's earlier, too, that there're couples making out, but... I think you'll always find couples against the wall or leaning up against a pillar... squeezing each other, like hugging or, sometimes you'll see them kind of like bumping their foreheads together lightly,

ACTRESS 4. ....I discovered this the other day, and what it was was, in almost every case, as far as the position of the couple, it'll be the guy who has his back against the wall, and the girl kind of pouring her weight into the guy... like oof, and they'll butt their heads together at regular intervals, oof oof... or maybe they're just frozen like that, and since I'm just walking by, I'm not sure of the exact timing but, sometimes they seem like they've lost their balance, or like, if the girl has her back against the wall with the guy... I don't think you see that very often but...

ACTRESS 4. ...But anyway I don't think you see that very often... is what I was thinking, but, you can never be sure, they could be in the opposite positions, and I actually did see one couple like that the other day, so now we're going to do the story about that,

ACTRESS 4. At Shinjuku Station, I ride the Odakyu line, so when I go to the station, at the West Entrance there's a regular Odakyu turnstile, but at the East Entrance, from the East Entrance if you want to get on the Odakyu, you buy the Odakyu ticket, and use it to go through the JR turnstile, right, and when you do that and go all the way to the far end where the Yamanote line and other lines are, there's a staircase going down near the West Entrance in front of which on the right hand side is the connecting turnstile for the Odakyu... so, I happened to be taking this route the other day, yesterday in fact, from the East Entrance, with my boyfriend, at the end of the day... we had made plans to eat lunch together so we met in the Alta before lunch and had stuffed cabbage for lunch, and then spent the rest of the day window shopping for clothes at the Isetan department store, I mean we didn't buy anything, and of course he wasn't really interested in it, and I knew that but kind of forced him to come with me... and we did a lot of other stuff before catching the last train... then at the end of the day, towards the end of our date, my boyfriend started saying he wanted to stop by the batting center near the East Entrance... you know, the batting center towards the back of Kabukicho, very conveniently located... so I just like watched him batting by himself as always, for a really long time,

ACTRESS 4. Oh, that's right, and I read this thing they had written there like Batting for Women, Towards a Slimmer Body, kind of poster inside, and I was like really? Does batting have that kind of result? And that made me want to try it, but I didn't then, because our time was almost up, but I was sure we'd be back here before long and I was determined to give it a try the next time... or like, recently, I've been trying to lose weight, I mean it's always been on my mind, but I always get coddled by my boyfriend... because he says stuff like, "What, you're fine just as you are, you're not fat at all," and like, "huh, I think plump girls are cuter anyway" but then I'm like, well which is it? ...But it turned out that he does prefer girls to be a little plump, and I say "turned out" in the past tense because... well basically he told me straight up the other day, "Up until recently I really preferred girls who have a little meat on their bones" and then, "but then I realized that what I was looking for in the plumpness was that when I touched a girl I could be like 'oh, she seemed really skinny, but actually there's still plenty going on' and if that's the case, I would actually prefer a skinny girl, you know, so now I am steadily making that shift"…and I was like when the hell did you have the opportunity that made you come to this realization?

(About this point in the script, **ACTRESS 1** *and* **ACTOR 3** *are noticeably in an embrace.)*

ACTRESS 4. …Right, so then, that also encouraged me to be in this phase now where I'm trying to lose weight, I've been thinking about secretly going by myself to one of the places that have bowling alleys and karaoke bars and skating and batting centers all in one in my neighborhood, just to try it out… right and so that day, after the batting center, we were getting close to the last train, so we decided to go home and we went home… and we thought we'd take the route I explained earlier, from the East Entrance, going through the JR turnstile heading for the Odakyu line… and that was when I saw these people, by the wall between the staircases leading up to the platforms, near the Yamanote or the Chuo line, around there… and at that moment, I was almost about to just walk past them, wondering whether these two were having a good time or whether they were having a fight, and I was really just glancing over at them but,

ACTOR 4. I could tell off the bat that they were totally making out but,

ACTRESS 4. …but, that's like, usually when you walk by something, you look at it and then forget about it, so I naturally assumed that I didn't know them, and I had no thoughts or reactions at all after we walked past them, so I was well on my way to forgetting about them completely… but then as we were entering the Odakyu line, my boyfriend said like, "hey, hey," he said, "you know those two who were hugging or like totally making out back there," he said, "the two of them work at my job," he said... huh, really, I thought,

ACTOR 4. Right, right, I mean up until that moment I had no idea they were an item, so when I saw him next, it was the next day, actually, because we had the same shift, I totally harassed him about it... and he was all, "What, you saw us? For real? You saw? Oh could you keep it on the down low, you know, at work, I mean I don't care all that much, but you know, Ogawa has, you know, a lot of history" he said,

ACTRESS 4. History? What history?

ACTOR 4. Well Ogawa, that's her name, she... right, right, what was the history,

ACTOR 4. ...No, but I was thinking I was really happy for Takeuchi to finally get a girlfriend... he didn't have one for a long time... so as his friend I did a lot of stuff to not help him out but just encourage him... so as part of those efforts... I mean it was really just two or three times... I invited him along to like a singles party?... basically, I was playing his trusty wingman,

ACTOR 4. ...Right, right, so that's not exactly right... what I mean is... it was that, you know there were a lot of people we went out with and she was one of the girls, you know... like what we were saying before, there was this girl who was super skinny, and the story there was that... like her wrists were so skinny you could grab them like this (*bringing his thumb and forefinger together*) probably, and her hips too like this (*with both hands*)... also she was tall like a model, and she let me touch her arm and stuff, and I was like, WHA- so skinny!... I thought, I thought that, but, at the same time, I thought that even such a skinny body has, what, a surprising sensation of flesh, that softness,... because up until then I always thought it would hurt to bump into someone really skinny and boney, like their bone might pierce into me, but then I realized

ACTOR 4. …but really Takeuchi's preference, we had talked about this kind of thing before, was for those super super skinny chicks… Right, so, I'd gotten into this interrogation with him, like doesn't it hurt to be with chicks that skinny, questions like that, and Takeuchi was like, Huh, Shimizu, it's actually not at all like the way you're imagining it, he said, and that's when I was like Ah- Takeuchi's had experience with this kind of thing, right right…

ACTOR 4. Right, that reminds me, the other day at our comic book cafe, we got a new part-timer, this guy named Miyata, and when I first saw him, I just assumed I thought he was like the same age as me and Takeuchi, so I was pretty chatty with him and trying to be friends with him, but then I saw his resume lying around in the office, and it said he was 32 years old … well he looks young… but I was like what the hell so you're on the MiKaKa side… so they've gained one, the MiKaKa… So with the addition of Miyata, they're now "MiMiKaKa" right?

ACTOR 4. …I guess it's obvious that I was trying to change the subject huh, sorry, sorry…

ACTOR 4. …but about Shimizu, see Shimizu takes really good care of his girlfriend, I mean, for example, like that teddy bear (*Rilakkuma*) she has is one thing, it's her birthday today, and he'd never forget that kind of thing, getting a really thoughtful birthday present… so when Shimizu found out that Takeuchi, about Takeuchi and Ogawa getting together, he was like, Oh that's what happened, that's awesome man, congratulations, he gave his, not advice, really, but some words about how he must absolutely do things like that, if he ever gets a girlfriend… or like, take this Rilakkuma… at first there was a teddy bear, that we saw before together at a store, and we got all excited about how so cute it was, so I was totally like, OK this year I'll get her that teddy bear, but the teddy bear, I didn't know until I tried to buy one, was like easily 10, 20, 30 thousand yen?! With their cute faces, at that price, that

was not going to work for me so… I ended up getting
that Rilakkuma which fell into the 3000 yen range…
but presents are not about monetary value, it's totally
about the feeling, and she was like wow, thank you!
wow I'm so happy, so I think she was pretty pleased
with it….

(pause)

ACTOR 3. …it's kind of a pretty ordinary thing to say but,
girlfriends are, great,…I mean, I was basically like this
but I was facing this way *(back turned towards audience)*
so I didn't realize that Shimizu had seen me at all,
so… Yeah, the fact is, that was actually our first date,
so we were just pure, not like going to the batting cage
like Shimizu and his girl… Yeah, we both had the day
off so we decided to meet up at Shinjuku, I mean why
Shinjuku of all places, go somewhere else on your day
off, right? but yeah, but we didn't really care where, we
just wanted to hang out with each other, so we ended
up picking Shinjuku… so we hung out like let's get a
coffee, let's get a bite, and spent the day together,

ACTOR 4. So basically both couples had spent the whole
day wandering around Shinjuku, and never ran into
each other, until the end of the day…

ACTOR 3. Right, small world… So, but ahhh it's almost the
last train…we were like let's hang out again soon, yeah,
and we'd been holding hands the entire day but, yeah,
but we hadn't gotten as close as we did at the station…
and at that moment, I was noticed how good Ogawa's
hair smelled, so I said, "Ogawa, yeah you smell so nice"

ACTRESS 1. Um… these are the kinds of stories that like
when other people hear them, they just seem like
dumb stories that are only special to you, but they're
actually totally lame and all the same but… I mean
I know that, but still… Right, when Takeuchi said
"Ogawa you smell so nice"… Um he was talking about
my hair, hmmm but I don't wear any perfume or anything, so that smell was probably just Pantene, I said,

but then Takeuchi got really serious and said, "No, it's not just that" and I was like, huh, what isn't just that? Like I didn't really get it but...

ACTOR 3. That's not it, "No, it's not just that" meant, sure, maybe the scent of Pantene was just the scent of Pantene, but Pantene alone couldn't have that kind of smell, I thought, and that's because Pantene and Ogawa's natural scent was yeah, mingled with Ogawa's natural scent, for the first time the Pantene reached its full scent potential in that mixture... that's what I meant by "No, it's not just that"

*(**ACTOR 3** and **ACTRESS 1** smell each other for a while. Then they stop.)*

ACTRESS 1. Huh, but Takeuchi actually you smell pretty nice yourself,

ACTOR 3. Ah, or like that's... at first I had like never been aware of deodorant-type products, but Shimizu is super on top of all that kind of stuff, so it was probably his influence on me that

ACTRESS 1. Yes

ACTOR 3. But this scent is just from the Febreze on my clothes

ACTRESS 1. ...Ah, yes, but that's totally OK I think... or like Febreze and Pantene are both made by Proctor and Gamble

ACTOR 3. Yeah... ah, oh right, oh right, Febreze,

(They start smelling each other again.)

ACTRESS 1. Is Shimizu's girlfriend someone at work, or like someone who used to work there?

ACTOR 3. I don't think so, I mean, no she's not... I mean I know but... yeah, she works somewhere else entirely like at a karaoke place or... yeah definitely it was a karaoke place,

ACTRESS 1. I'm a little curious about what kind of person Shimizu's girlfriend is like, but

ACTOR 3. Oh, really?

ACTRESS 1. Yes,

ACTOR 3. That was because we'd said maybe all four of us should go out to karaoke? And if that's the case... we could probably get into the karaoke place where she works with a discount, Shimizu had said, because my girlfriend works at a karaoke place, right, right

ACTRESS 1. Oh, then that's super we should all get together there

ACTOR 3. Yeah

ACTRESS 1. ...and then, pretty soon a few days after, the four of us went to the karaoke place... and I'm sure it was then that I understood right away when I saw her that Shimizu's girlfriend was really in love with Shimizu... when the two boys went to the bathroom, and they were gone for a long time and we were both like when are they coming back... but that was actually, before the karaoke, we had gone to a bar, and it was like three thousand a head, and the boys especially had drunk a lot, so at that moment the two boys were, both of them were barfing in the bathroom, apparently, which is what I learned later, but at the time we were like, they sure are taking a long time... so during that pretty long stretch of time, it was just me and Shimizu's girlfriend... and it so happened that we'd just finished a song, and we hadn't programmed the next song in the queue so the machine was stopped, right, and just from the room down the hall we could hear this person singing horribly... so that was when I was asking Shimizu's girlfriend all these questions about how they'd gotten together and I was like Oh that's how you met, and Oh you've been together for that long? And the thing that surprised me the most was I asked Shimizu's girlfriend how old she was and she said 30, and I was like no way, you don't look it, I thought you were like 20, I was really surprised, but of course saying I thought she was 20 was an exaggeration but...

ACTRESS 1. ...also, what I thought was so cute about Shimizu's girlfriend was... I mean the story was... Shimizu's girlfriend was telling me how much she really really liked him, Shimizu, and how when they were together just the two of them, that was all she needed, and like... Shimizu and his girlfriend both still live with their parents but, I mean for now anything else is out of the question so, but, apparently they'd been talking about how great it would be if they could one day live together, were able to live together, and she was saying how much she loved talking about that with him... that's when I feel it the most, that wow I am really in love with Shimizu... I really hope that it happens, one day, just the two of us forever, even into our old age, to go on and on.... like that's such a, they write songs about that kind of thing, like totally predictable cheesy love songs, for sure... But that's how we still feel and think about each other, and we talk about it, that we wish we could be together forever and ever, we really believe it,

ACTRESS 1. ...When we're together, I really think that's all I need, what I mean is, the words come out sounding totally trite but, I really really think so,

ACTRESS 1. "The words come out sounding totally trite," I said, but I was actually thinking how extraordinary this feeling is, like don't lump me with anyone else who thinks they can express their feelings with words, like the way I felt is so extraordinary there's no way ordinary words can capture how I feel, but then when you think about all the other people in the world who have used these words throughout history, and their feelings, perhaps each and every one of them was experiencing as profound an emotion as I was, actually... and if so, then these trite words, I wish it could just be the two of us forever, that's all I need, maybe these words are actually enough,

(ACTRESS 1 *and* ACTOR 3 *embrace and lean in to kiss, but sense something and suddenly sniff at each other. After a while, a homeless person crosses in front of them.*)

END OF PLAY

OTHER TITLES AVAILABLE FROM SAMUEL FRENCH

STROM THURMOND IS NOT A RACIST

Thomas Bradshaw

Satire / 5m, 2f (doubling, flexible casting possible) / Modular sets

Inspired by a true story, *Strom Thurmond is Not a Racist* is an absurdist look at the life of Senator Strom Thurmond. After fathering a child with his black maid as a young man, the extremely white Strom Thurmond became one of the country's greatest segregationists; all the while playing daddy to his bi-racial daughter Essie Mae Washington Williams. How could someone live such a duplicitous life? It happens. Winner of The American Theater Coop's National Playwriting Contest in 2005. Published with *Cleansed*.

This play contains mature language and situations.

"Tom Bradshaw's most important contribution to society is snatching narrative and its elements back from the clutches of the ordinary."
– Richard Maxwell, Playwright and Director

"Bradshaw has a positive genius for explosive imagery, putting biracial Lauraul in a Klan costume and penning a demonic parody of Martin Luther King's "I Have A Dream" speech for Strom Thurmond….Bradshaw has a deep dramatic and linguistic intelligence."
– *Village Voice*

"These uncomfortably intense plays focus on racism in our society, from the Dixiecrats of the south to the confused generation of today. The intensity that Bradshaw intended came through tenfold."
– *New York Cool*

OTHER TITLES AVAILABLE FROM SAMUEL FRENCH

WE ARE NOT THESE HANDS

Sheila Callaghan

Comedy / 1m, 2f / Simple set

Ever since their school blew up, Moth and Belly have taken to stalking an illegal internet café in the hopes of one day being allowed in. They take particular interest in Leather, a skittish older man doing research in the café.

Leather is a self-proclaimed "freelance scholar" from a foreign land with a sketchy past and a sticky secret. Leather begins to fall head over heals in love with Moth... but what about Belly? This play explores the effects of rampant capitalism on a country that is ill-prepared for it.

"Bold and engaging, *We Are Not These Hands* is as fun as it is engaging...Rich in detail and full of humor and pathos."
– *Oakland Tribune*

"Swaggering eccentricity...Callaghan takes a lavish mud bath in a broken language...Ripe apocalyptic slang; at its best, it's racy and unrefined, the kind of stuff you might imagine kids in the back alleys of a decaying world might sling around."
– *The Washington Post*

"The gap between rich and poor yawns so wide it aches in Sheila Callaghan's *We Are Not These Hands*, but much of the ache is from laughter. Hands is a comically engaging, subversively penetrating look at the human cost of unbridled capitalism on both sides of the river...the anger of the play's social vision is partly concealed by its copious humor, emerging more forcefully after it's over...*Hands* bristles with bright, comic originality, particularly in depicting the limitations of its people."
– *San Francisco Chronicle*

OTHER TITLES AVAILABLE FROM SAMUEL FRENCH

A VERY MERRY UNAUTHORIZED CHILDREN'S SCIENTOLOGY PAGEANT

Kyle Jarrow

Musical / 5m, 5f (Doubling possible) / Interior

A jubilant cast of children celebrate the controversial religion in uplifting pageantry and song. The actual teachings of The Church of Scientology are explained and dissected against the candy-colored backdrop of a traditional nativity play. *Pageant* is a musical biography of the life of L. Ron Hubbard, with child-friendly explanations of Hubbard's notion of the divided mind (embodied by the lovely identical twins Emma and Sophie Whitfield in matching brain outfits) and a device called the e-meter (or electropsychometer), used to monitor the human psyche, which is demonstrated by stick puppets. Grade school children, portraying Tom Cruise, Kirstie Alley, John Travolta, and other less starry Scientologists, brings the controversial Church of Scientology to jubilant life in story and song.

CPSIA information can be obtained at www.ICGtesting.com
Printed in the USA
BVOW10s0838120914

366216BV00011B/370/P